What's Your Style?

Alison Bell

Let's Party!

Lobster Press™

Let's Party!
Text © 2005 Alison Bell
Illustrations © 2005 Kun-Sung Chung

Published by Lobster Press™
1620 Sherbrooke Street West, Suites C & D
Montréal, Québec H3H 1C9
Tel. (514) 904-1100 • Fax (514) 904-1101
www.lobsterpress.com

Publisher: Alison Fripp
Editors: Alison Fripp & Karen Li
Cover & Book Design: Olena Lytvyn
Production Manager: Tammy Desnoyers

Library and Archives Canada Cataloguing in Publication

Bell, Alison
       Let's party! / Alison Bell ; Kun-Sung Chung, illustrator.

(What's your style?)
ISBN 1-894222-99-7

       1. Parties--Juvenile literature. 2. Entertaining--Juvenile literature.
3. Handicraft for girls--Juvenile literature. I. Chung, Kun-Sung, 1971- II.
Title. III. Series.

GV1205.B44 2005   j793.2'1   C2005-900886-5

The activities in this book have been tested and are safe when conducted as instructed. The author and publisher accept no responsibility for any damage caused or sustained by the use or misuse of ideas or material featured in *Let's Party!*

Palm Pilot is a trademark of 3Com Corporation; **GameBoy** is a registered trademark of Nintendo Corporation; **7 UP** is a trademark of Dr Pepper/Seven Up, Inc.; **Cool Whip**, **Life Savers**, and **Jell-O** are trademarks of Kraft Foods, Inc.; **M&M's** and **Skittles** are trademarks of Mars, Inc.; **Reese's Pieces** is a trademark of The Hershey Company; **Tupperware** is a trademark of Tupperware Company; **Polaroid** is a trademark of Polaroid Corporation; **Bundt** is a trademark of Robin Hood Multifoods, Inc.; **Smarties** is a trademark of Société des Produits Nestlé S.A; **Zinka** is a trademark of Zinka, Inc.

Printed and bound in China.

TABLE OF Contents

To my daughter, Libby.
—Alison BELL

Introduction

Planning a party? Stressing out because you can't come up with a creative idea for a cool get-together?

NO PROBLEM! What's Your Style? *Let's Party!* offers eight concrete and complete party plans that tap into the latest trends and are guaranteed to be a hit with your guests. First, take a quiz to discover your Party Profile and learn how your party habits are an expression of your personality. Then pick and choose from the different party ideas to put on an unforgettable get-together.

The chapters are jam-packed with fun decorating, food, and music ideas, as well as innovative party activities. You'll also find survival tactics tailored to your own personality and eight mini-quizzes that test your party subject IQ. In addition, you'll get a crash course in Hostessing 101, with dozens of practical tips ranging from how to word your invitations to how to say goodbye to that lingering guest who just won't leave!

With so many options, your parties will never be less than spectacular. The only question left is: How soon can you throw the next one?

Chapter 1

WHAT'S *Your* STYLE?

Whether you throw tons of get-togethers or only one in a blue moon, you can always put your own stamp on the gatherings you host. What type of person are you, and how is this reflected in your Party Personality?

Take this quiz to find out!

1 Your idea of the perfect party is...

a. a carefully choreographed event jam-packed with activities.

b. a loose affair where not much is planned.

c. a roomful of happy guests and good conversation.

d. a once-in-a-lifetime event no one will ever forget!

2 You prefer parties that are...

a. small—a large group can get too rowdy.

b. not too small, because then everyone will notice when you show up late!

c. large—you like to see as many of your friends as possible.

d. mega-huge. You love events that are over the top!

3 When it comes time to plan the menu for your party, you...

a. diligently test out every recipe beforehand to make sure those double fudge brownies are double delish and not double trouble!

b. wing it until the last minute— who knows what you'll feel like serving until a day or two before the party?

c. ask your friends what their favorite foods are and make sure to have them on hand.

d. track down the most obscure recipes you can find. Cajun-fried catfish with chocolate sauce, anyone?

4 The one thing you can't live without is...

a. your organizer.

b. your spontaneity.

c. your friends.

d. your big ideas!

5 Which of the following are you most likely to carry in your purse?

a. Just the essentials—a wallet, comb, and lipgloss.

b. A mad jumble of junk.

c. A cell phone with text messaging.

d. Something eclectic—a book of obscure poetry and juggling balls.

6 At a party, you're most likely to be found...

a. talking to one or two close friends.

b. chatting with whoever happens to be sitting next to you.

c. working the room.

d. causing a scene!

7 When it comes to your to-do list, you...

a. usually get 99 percent of it accomplished each day.

b. what to-do list?

c. complete only the items that involve friends.

d. will never get through it, unless you've won an Academy award and eliminated world hunger!

8 Time to get out those party invitations. You...

a. send them out a month in advance—you can't rest until they're in the mail.

b. wait until a day or two before the party, then call or e-mail your guests.

c. mail them out three weeks in advance, just like the etiquette books advise.

d. hand-deliver them with a flourish.

9 It's Saturday morning. You tend to roll out of bed...

a. when the alarm goes off at 6:30 a.m., same time as during the week.

b. around noon.

c. whenever the first friend calls or text messages.

d. who says you ever went to sleep?

10 A big test is coming up. You...

a. make up a study schedule weeks in advance and color code all your notes for easy reference.

b. start studying the night before—hey, that way all the info is "fresh" in your mind.

c. organize a study group so you and your pals can hit the books together.

d. protest. Hasn't your teacher heard? Tests are a totally bogus way to evaluate progress.

11 At the last minute, a friend tells you she's bringing her three cousins to your party. You...

a. freak! You're not prepared to handle three extra guests.

b. shrug. No biggie!

c. think up a good icebreaker to make sure the cousins meet everyone and feel at ease.

d. figure it's a good excuse to broaden the party and ask all the guests to bring along a friend or two.

12 You're in charge of a big school project. You...

a. do 99 percent of the work yourself.

b. delegate, delegate, delegate.

c. enlist the help of your good friends to lend you a hand.

d. spend so much time arguing over the merit of the project that it's given to someone else.

13 During one of your parties, your parents stick too close. You...

a. are secretly happy. They can help keep everything running smoothly.

b. figure, no problemo! You're very tolerant of the parental units.

c. tactfully ask them to retreat to their bedroom because they're cramping your guests' style.

d. give them an emotional plea worthy of an Oscar on why you and your friends need space!

14 When it comes to RSVPing to parties, you...

a. respond the day you get the invitation.

b. just show up. RSVPing is so not necessary!

c. RSVP within the time frame stated on the invitation.

d. show off your creativity by responding with a poem or a song.

15 You have a free Sunday afternoon. You plan on...

a. cleaning out your closet (again!).

b. doing nothing.

c. hanging out with your buddies.

d. brainstorming ways to help the local homeless.

16 The perfect length of any party you throw is...

a. three hours tops—you like to keep them short and sweet.

b. as long as everyone wants to stay.

c. whatever length Miss Manners recommends.

d. ultra-long. Marathon parties are the only way to go!

17 It's your best friend's birthday. For a present, you...

a. give her something practical.

b. give her an IOU for the gift you *meant* to buy but never got around to purchasing.

c. get her something she's been really wanting.

d. get her dozens of presents wrapped in a sea of bows and ribbons.

How did you score? Turn the page to find out!

7

control chick

If being organized were an Olympic sport, you'd take the gold medal in every event. You're detail-minded, punctual, and responsible. You are a perfectionist and love to plan ahead so you'll know exactly what to expect. Your friends marvel at how you can get so much done every day.

YOUR MOTTO: "Give me a to-do list or give me death."

ON YOUR MOST-LIKED LIST: Programmable watches, palm pilots, perfectly made beds, highlighter pens, an organized closet, alphabetized CD collections, new textbooks, a clean desk.

ON YOUR HIT LIST: Friends who are late, messy lockers, disorganized teachers, wasting time standing in line, breaking rules, kids who get into trouble, surprises.

WHAT FRIENDS DON'T KNOW ABOUT YOU: Yes, you can kick back and relax...after you've made sure that you've got the situation totally under control, that is.

FUTURE FORECAST: Donald Trump, watch out! With your organizational skills and dedication to hard work, you're bound to shoot straight to the top in any career.

YOUR PARTY PROFILE: You start planning your parties months in advance and spend hours poring over magazines, cookbooks, and hostess guides to cull the very best ideas. You schedule party activities down to the minute and are irked when things get off track. You prefer to handle all the details on your own; frankly, you know you can trust yourself to get things done, but you can't say the same for everyone else. Once the party's over, you'll do a postmortem to see what, if any, improvements are needed next time around.

If you answered mainly b s, you're an

improv queen

You're easygoing and relaxed. You live for the moment. A creative thinker, you love to daydream and need lots of time to just "be." Rather than spend your time and energy planning events, you prefer to just show up and have fun. You also have a lot of interests and are easily distracted, which might explain why you tend to procrastinate on everything from schoolwork to cleaning up your room. But because you're a true free spirit, leaving things to the last minute doesn't bother you a bit!

YOUR MOTTO: "Don't worry. Be happy."

ON YOUR MOST-LIKED LIST: Flexible deadlines, a sketch-book, daydreaming, friends with lively imaginations, spontaneous decisions, new hobbies, traveling, a messy room.

ON YOUR HIT LIST: Deadlines, clocks, routines, uptight people, sterile environments, neat freaks, day planners, having to read instructions, big books filled with small type.

WHAT FRIENDS DON'T KNOW ABOUT YOU: You might act like you hate it when they try to get you organized. But, deep down, you're thankful; even you know you could use some structure in your life!

FUTURE FORECAST: You will flourish in any field where your creativity can run free!

YOUR PARTY PROFILE: Details be darned! You'd rather let your party evolve naturally than do a lot of advanced organizing. Sure, you have a general idea of what will happen, but you want lots of wiggle room for spontaneity. Plus, all that pre-planning can be a big drag. One thing's for sure: your party will be an absolute blast because fun is your top priority. And the best thing about being the hostess? You can't be late because you live there!

If you answered mainly C s, you're a

hostess with the mostess

You're socially savvy and always seem to know the right thing to say at the right time. You're loyal, considerate, and empathetic. You are a good listener, and you love to be "in the know." Friends are everything to you, which is why you're such a popular gal!

YOUR MOTTO: "You gotta have friends."

ON YOUR MOST-LIKED LIST: Text messaging, e-mail, passing notes in class, heart-to-heart chats, helping others, good manners, group projects, talk radio, meeting new people, being on teams, celebrity magazines.

ON YOUR HIT LIST: Unreturned e-mails, game boys and computer games (too isolating), rude people, solo projects, cell phone dead zones, getting stuck talking to just one person at a party.

WHAT FRIENDS DON'T KNOW ABOUT YOU: Yes, you actually do need some down time now and then to recharge your social batteries, or else you can get a little testy. (So that explains those rare times you actually turn down an invitation!)

FUTURE FORECAST: You're a natural in any field where you can use your amazing people skills.

YOUR PARTY PROFILE: When you throw a party, you make sure to give each guest your full attention. If everyone isn't having a good time, you can't either. You devour any party etiquette books ahead of time and are a genius at making everyone feel at ease. As a hostess, you face only one dilemma: where to cut off the guest list! You have so many friends that it could go on forever!

If you answered mainly d**s, you're an**

over-the-top gal

You're passionate, emotional, idealistic, and brimming with big ideas. You're a true original who hates to be one of the crowd. You're dramatic and love big gestures. For example, instead of sending your mom a couple of flowers for Mother's Day, you shower her with two dozen roses! And one thing's for sure, you charge anything you're involved in with full-wattage energy!

YOUR MOTTO: "Go for it!"

ON YOUR MOST-LIKED LIST: Breaking rules, taking risks, wearing bright colors, loud music, esoteric books, volunteering, ethnic foods, different cultures, speaking up for what you believe in.

ON YOUR HIT LIST: Vanilla ice cream, bland people, authority figures, thinking small, ruts, mainstream culture, hiding your true feelings, prejudice, injustice.

WHAT FRIENDS DON'T KNOW ABOUT YOU: Because you come off as larger than life and invulnerable, friends might think they can tell you anything and you won't flinch. Not true! Deep down, you are just as sensitive as the next gal.

FUTURE FORECAST: You're a visionary and have the energy and will to change the world for the better.

YOUR PARTY PROFILE: If big is good, bigger is even better. You aim to throw an unforgettable party that goes over the top in every way. For example, if most people give out one party favor, you want to hand out dozens. You just wish you had the budget to fulfill your party dreams—like flying everyone over to Spain to watch the running of the bulls. But even on less, your parties are legendary and have people talking for months!

Chapter 2

THE SENSATIONAL Spa PARTY

GIRLS DON'T JUST want to have fun…they want to be pampered, too! Give each guest the royal treatment with an afternoon filled with manicures, pedicures, and soothing facials. Her inner princess will glow, and so will yours. But you'll only have yourself to blame if everyone is so relaxed that no one wants leave at the end of the day!

CHECKLIST TO SUCCESS

✓ **Three weeks before the party,** print and send out your invitations. (Page 14)

✓ **One week before the party,** ask your friends or neighbors if you may borrow their blenders for the big day. Shop for all spa items, e.g. cotton balls, paper towels, nail polish remover, etc. (Pages 14 & 17)

✓ **Two days before the party,** pick up the blenders. Do all the food shopping for your lunch and home-made beauty treatments. (Pages 15 & 16)

✓ **The day before the party,** bake or buy the brownies. Set up the beauty stations. (Pages 14)

✓ **The morning of the party,** make the salad and sandwiches. Refrigerate. Make the beauty treatments. Refrigerate. (Pages 15 & 16)

✓ **Right before the guests arrive,** take the homemade beauty treatments out of the refrigerator. Set out the perishable smoothie ingredients at a "smoothie bar."

Now your spa is open and ready for business!

WHAT'S *your* BEAUTY IQ?

Spa living is all about feeling and looking your best. But how much do you really know about beauty basics? Take this quickie quiz to find out.

1 A loofah is…
- **a.** a new dance move.
- **b.** an ingredient in shampoo that makes your hair super silky.
- **c.** a natural body sponge.

2 What's a T-zone?
- **a.** The line football players run over to score a touchdown.
- **b.** An imaginary line running between your shoulders and chest.
- **c.** An imaginary line running between your eyebrows and down your nose.

3 Pimples can be caused by…
- **a.** being around other kids with breakouts—they're contagious, aren't they?
- **b.** eating greasy foods and chocolate.
- **c.** boy woes and other stressors.

4 If you want to lose— and keep off—weight…
- **a.** buy the most recent and trendiest diet book, and follow it religiously!
- **b.** easy—eat nothing!
- **c.** eat a nutritious diet filled with fruits & vegetables, exercise regularly, and drink a lot of water.

5 What is Reiki?
- **a.** The new anime on TV.
- **b.** Muscle-pounding massage.
- **c.** A healing therapy based on the channeling of energies.

6 If a makeup or skin care product is labeled noncomedogenic, it means…
- **a.** it's not for use on animals.
- **b.** it hasn't been tested on animals.
- **c.** it's non-acne forming.

7 What does TM stand for?
- **a.** Transcendental medication.
- **b.** Transatlantic meltdown.
- **c.** Transcendental meditation.

8 What is the best beauty tip of all?
- **a.** Wear tons of makeup and skin care products.
- **b.** Make sure you're on top of every fad and trend.
- **c.** Smile! This is when your inner beauty really shines!

Answers:
The correct answer for each question is C.

Read on for more sensational spa information!

13

You have been booked for an appointment at

Elizabeth's Elegant

Escape & Spa

1234 Main St.

Your appointment time:
Saturday, March 2, 12 – 3 p.m.

Services provided include:
Homemade Beauty Treatments
Manicure & Pedicure
Smoothie Sampler

Lunch will be served.
Prepare to be pampered like never before!
RSVP to Spa Manager Elizabeth Jones
777-7777 or e-mail Lizjones@home.com

LET'S GET IT Started!

The Invites

HERE'S AN IDEA for one-of-a-kind invitations: write up or use a computer to create a fake spa brochure listing all the services your guests will receive at the party. Come up with a name for your spa, such as "Elizabeth's Elegant Escape and Spa." Substitute the starting time of the party with "appointment time."

◀ Here's a sample invitation you can follow.

RSVP

The Setting

TURN YOUR HOME into several different beauty stations where girls can rotate from one spa experience to another. While a few girls are getting manicures and pedicures, another group can be getting facials, and so on.

To make sure everyone gets her share of services, split your guests up into groups of two or three (depending on the number of guests) so that they can work on each other as they rotate from station to station. After all, when you're among friends, it's just as much fun to give as it is to get a little pampering!

One area of your home that you will definitely use is the kitchen, so make sure it's ready to receive guests. Some miscellaneous items you might want to have on hand are:

- cloth and paper towels to mop up any accidental spills.
- ponytail holders so your guests can pull their hair back before getting their facials.
- cleansing cloths so party-goers can remove any makeup before testing the treatments.
- cotton balls and swabs to fix up any application errors.

TiP from an OVeR-the-Top gal

Did you plan too many beauty stations or invite too many guests? One good way to keep the activities moving is to enlist the help of family members (such as your mom, sister, or aunt) to give your guests their treatments. Pay your helpers back with a one-on-one, full spa treatment at the end of the day!

The Edibles

smoothie sampler

SMOOTHIES ARE a healthy spa treat. Want to know the "recipe" for a delicious homemade smoothie? Take 2 cups of almost any fruit, add 1 cup of "thickener" (such as yogurt or ice cream) and 1 cup of juice or milk. Blend it all together, and you have one sensational smoothie.

Borrow one or two extra blenders from a neighbor or friend (the blenders will come in handy when preparing spa treatments, too!), and let your guests make their own concoctions. Here are a few ingredients to have on hand. (If the fruit you crave isn't in season, just use the frozen kind.)

Fruits: strawberries, blueberries, raspberries, pineapple, mangoes, kiwis, peaches, and bananas.

Liquids: milk, soy milk, apple juice, orange juice, and pineapple juice.

Optional: ice, honey, sugar, cinnamon, and peanut butter.

Throw all or some of the above ingredients in a blender and see how they taste! Pour samples into small cups so everyone can try all the yummy combinations.

In addition to the smoothies, serve up some small, spa-like sandwiches, sans crust. ▼

cucumber tea sandwiches

You'll need:
- 2 cucumbers, peeled, very thinly sliced
- 1 stick butter, room temperature
- 1 cup chopped watercress leaves
- 8 slices white bread
- salt to taste

BUTTER THE BREAD and sprinkle some watercress leaves on top. Add cucumber slices and a dash of salt. Cut the crusts from the bread. Next, cut the sandwiches diagonally. Cut them diagonally in half again. The result: 32 triangle-shaped quarters.

To round out the menu, serve a simple garden salad and some decadent brownies for dessert!

The Playlist

TURN ON SOME soothing tunes—anything from jazz (Miles Davis, Thelonious Monk, Billie Holiday, or Duke Ellington) to classical music (try recordings of Bach's "Cello Suites," Satie's "Piano Works," or the quieter compositions of Mozart or Beethoven). Or, pop in some New age tunes or Ambient music. Even Gregorian chants will do the trick! Just think calm and serene when picking out music for your party playlist.

Tip from an IMPROV Queen

If your guests are more of a PB & J crowd than tea sandwich connoisseurs, simply make a bunch of sandwiches, cut the crusts off, and cut into triangles. Any sandwich cut this way has that special spa style!

HOMEMADE
Beauty

THESE CONCOCTIONS are easy to whip up and will leave everyone's complexion glowing. Make them the day of the party so they'll be fresh. The recipes below are enough for three to four people, so double or triple the amounts as needed. These recipes do not contain preservatives, so discard leftover treatments after the party.

super sugar scrub

This little scrub is a great pick-me-up for your skin. It also works as an exfoliant, removing dead skin cells from your face.

Pour the sugar into a small plastic container. Bury the beans in the sugar. Seal the container. Within minutes, the sugar will have a fab vanilla scent.

To apply, mix the scrub with some liquid cleanser or warm water. Spread the mixture on your face, gently massaging your skin for a minute. Wash off with warm water.

You'll need:
- 1 cup sugar
- 4 or 5 vanilla coffee beans (available in bulk at most markets)

cucumber kiwi cooler

Smooth a little of this on your face for a tingly, cool feeling! This toner removes any dirt or old cleanser from your skin while tightening your pores.

Use a blender to liquefy all ingredients. Strain out the solids with a sieve.

Pour some of the mixture on a cotton ball and smooth all over your face. After a minute, rinse off with warm water.

You'll need:
- 1 cucumber, chopped
- 1 kiwi, chopped
- 1 tsp fresh mint leaves
- 1 cup distilled or purified water

banana fo-fanna face masque

Put this on for smooth, moist skin. (If you have super oily skin and are prone to breakouts, skip this masque.)

In a small bowl, mash the banana with a fork until smooth. Add the honey and mix well.

Massage the banana mixture gently onto your face. Place a slice of cucumber over each eye to soothe and reduce puffiness in the eye area. Leave masque on for ten minutes, and then wash off with warm water.

You'll need:
- 1 ripe banana
- 1 tsp honey
- cooled cucumber slices (optional)

TiP from a HOSTess with the MOSTess

Find out beforehand if any of your guests have food or skin allergies. Nothing ruins a day at the spa like a head-to-toe rash!

QUICK 'N EASY
Manicures & Pedicures

YOUR GUESTS will leave your home with two perfect sets of ten—great looking toes and fingernails! First, make sure you have all the tools of the trade. ▶

To give a manicure or pedicure:

1. Saturate cotton balls in polish remover and remove any old polish.
2. Clean dirt from under nails with a cotton swab.
3. Using an emery board, file fingernails into an oval shape. Toenails should be filed straight across. (Tip: File nails in one direction only. Filing them back and forth can damage the nail.)
4. Apply a base coat and let dry.
5. Apply two coats of polish. For perfect polishing, think three, as in three strokes: paint one stroke down the middle of your nail, followed by one stroke on either side.
6. Apply a top coat and let dry.
7. Remove any stray polish with a cotton swab dipped in polish remover. Press on the nail decals. Now flash those nails for the world to see, because, hands (and feet!) down, they look fab!

manicure & pedicure basics

- Polish remover
- Emery boards (For the sake of hygiene, provide each guest with her own.)
- Toenail separators (optional)
- Base coat
- Nail polish (For a variety of colors, ask each guest to bring polishes from home to share.)
- Top coat
- Cotton balls & swabs
- Paper towels
- Nail decals (for fun!)

SAYING Goodbye

BEFORE THE PARTY, buy some inexpensive makeup bags at the drugstore, along with some beauty essentials (tweezers, scented soap, etc.) to go in them. Make each girl a beauty bag, and hand it to her as she leaves. Don't forget to book an "appointment" for your next spa date—next year on your birthday, perhaps?

Chapter 3

THE Freaky Fortune Teller's PARTY

READY TO GET OUT A CRYSTAL BALL (metaphorically speaking) and see what the future holds for your friends? Will they live long, productive lives? Be happy in love? Have lots of children? Or be total career divas? Find out together when you throw a forward-looking party that gives guests a glimpse of what tomorrow has in store!

CHECKLIST TO SUCCESS

✓ **Three weeks before the party, print and send out your invitations.** While you're on the computer, print out your fake fortunes and your Chinese Zodiac place cards, too. (Page 20)

✓ **Three days before the party, find and decorate a coffee can for the time capsule.** (Page 23)

✓ **Two days before the party, do all the shopping for the Mandarin Orange Salad.** Pick up some fortune cookies and loose-leaf tea. If you need them, buy some candles and incense, too! (Page 21)

✓ **The day before the party, un-stuff the fortune cookies.** Re-stuff them with your own fortunes.

✓ **The morning of the party, decorate the house.** Make your salad. Refrigerate. Don't add the dressing until you are ready to serve the salad, though!

✓ **Right before your guests arrive, order the takeout** (specifying when you want the food delivered). Dim the lights. Light your candles and incense to create a supernatural atmosphere.

WHAT'S *your* ASTROLOGICAL IQ?

Many people look to the stars to learn their future. How much do you and your pals really know about astrology? Find out with this quickie quiz.

1 How many signs are there in the Zodiac?

a. 12
b. 10
c. 6

2 The signs of the Zodiac relate to which heavenly body?

a. The sun
b. The moon
c. The planet Neptune

3 The symbol for Pisces is...

a. two fish.
b. the ram.
c. the crab.

4 Which of all the signs would most likely be a neat freak?

a. Virgo
b. Gemini
c. Cancer

5 The word astrology comes from the ancient...

a. Greeks and Romans.
b. Chinese.
c. Egyptians.

6 Usher's birthday is October 14. This makes him a...

a. Libra.
b. Sagittarius.
c. Capricorn.

7 Which sign is associated with stubbornness?

a. Taurus
b. Libra
c. Cancer

8 Each astrological sign reflects one of these four elements:

a. Water, Air, Fire, or Earth.
b. Metal, Ore, Gold, or Silver.
c. Water, Metal, Fire, Gold.

Would you call this girl a Pisces?

Answers:
The correct answer for each question is a.

Read on to find out more freaky fortune-telling facts!

Cancer

Taurus

Capricorn

Libra

Sagittarius

19

In your future, I see...

A Fabulous Party!

Given By: Elizabeth Jones

When: 6-9 p.m.
Saturday, March 2

Where: 1234 Main Street

The theme:
Fortune-Telling!

RSVP: Try telepathy.
If that doesn't work,
call or e-mail Elizabeth.
777-7777 or Lizjones@home.com

LET'S GET IT Started!

The Invites

NOTHING SAYS FORTUNE-TELLING like a crystal ball. Try drawing or downloading an image of one from your computer to frame the details of the party. Offer your guests a prediction that their futures hold "a very special party." Then give all the details. Plan the party during the evening—the darkness lends itself to an otherworldly vibe!
◀ Here's a sample invitation you can follow.

The Setting

SET THE MOOD BY DIMMING THE LIGHTS in your home. Or, if your lights don't have dimmers, turn off all bright overhead lights and use only smaller lamps. Light some candles (keep them up high so they won't get knocked over), and get into the cosmic mood by burning some incense. Cut out pictures of moons, suns, and stars, and hang them from the ceiling or furniture with ribbons.

Have some flowing scarves on hand to drape over the backs of chairs and lay across tables. This and any other romantic or exotic paraphernalia will also help you and your guests look the part of bona fide fortune-tellers: you can take the scarves and tie them around your heads or hips when it comes time to read one another's palms!

The Playlist

AS GUESTS ENTER, play "Que Sera, Sera" by Doris Day. "Sister Psychic" by Smash Mouth is also a natural choice, as are any of the haunting songs by Train, such as "Calling All Angels." In addition, any songs from the mystical Irish singer Enya will help set an otherworldly mood. And music by the Cocteau Twins will also contribute to the ethereal ambiance. Albums to try: *Head over Heels* and *Treasure*.

20

The Edibles

COMPLEMENT YOUR fortune-telling theme with a menu inspired by the Far East. Prepare a Mandarin Orange Salad served with fortune cookies and loose-leaf tea (for tea leaf readings, of course!). Round out the meal by ordering Chinese takeout and set place cards at the table with each guest's Chinese Zodiac sign.

雞

You'll need:

- 6 cups salad greens
- 1 can mandarin oranges
- 1/4 red onion, thinly sliced
- 1 cup cubed cooked chicken (optional)
- sliced almonds (optional)

mandarin orange salad

Wash the salad greens, and drain the mandarin oranges, discarding the juice. Mix the first four ingredients, and serve with Orange Balsamic Dressing. Sprinkle the sliced almonds on top of the salad as garnish.

orange balsamic dressing

Pour oil into a bowl. Mix in remaining ingredients. Toss dressing with salad. Serve.

You'll need:

- 1/2 cup olive oil
- 1/4 cup orange juice
- 1 tbsp grated orange peel
- 3 tbsp balsamic vinegar
- 1 tsp ground cumin
- salt to taste

tea time

Serve tea with your cookies so your guests can read the leaves. Here's how to try your hand at this ancient art:

Steep the tea in a pot using loose tea leaves. Pour the tea into cups, making sure some tea leaves get into every cup. As you drink the tea, think of a question you'd like answered. When you've finished, swirl the cup three times in your left hand, and then turn the cup onto a saucer so the leaves fall out. The shapes that appear will symbolically answer your question. For example, a heart shape means love. And leaves grouped to resemble an animal may be a stand-in for your beloved dog, Shep.

For dessert, hand out personalized fortune cookies. Use tweezers to pull out the original fortunes, and then re-stuff the cookies with fortunes that you've written yourself.

▼ A few fortune ideas:

TiP from a HOSTESS with the MOSTESS

Some fortune cookies are sealed too tightly, and it will be impossible to tweeze fortunes in or out. If this happens, put the alternative fortunes in a bowl so your guests can reach for their fortunes instead of cracking them out of the cookies.

Smile! Soon those pearly whites will be covered with braces.

Pucker up! Your first kiss is coming.

Oh dear. Your dog really does eat your homework!

GAMES &
Activities

Palm reading

FOR CENTURIES, people have believed that our hands tell volumes about our personalities. What do your guests' hands reveal? Learn all about the basics of palm reading, and then let your friends try reading each other's hands!

But which hand should you read? Palm readers read the dominant hand. In other words, if you're right-handed, read your right hand. Why? The non-dominant hand tells what talents, skills, and potentials you're born with. The dominant hand reveals what you will actually do with your gifts!

To find out more about palm reading, check out the following books before your party:

• **Discover Yourself Through Palm Reading: Learning How to Read Yourself and Your Future, Line by Line** by R. Robinson.
• **The Complete Idiot's Guide to Palmistry** by R. Gile and L. Lenard.

Follow that line!

OUR PALMS HAVE THREE main lines: the life line, the heart line, and the head line.

the life line

Palm readers believe that life lines don't tell us how long we'll live, but how well we'll live.

• A long, deep life line foretells a life full of energy, productivity, and good health.
• A short, weak line may mean that you're on the timid side.
• A line that splits in two shows a crossroad at some point in your life. You'll have to decide which "path" to take.

the head line

The head line represents our logic and intelligence.

• A clear, deep line reveals—you've got it—that you're a clear, deep thinker!
• A faint line means you have a hard time concentrating!
• If the line forks at the end (under your pinkie), you're blessed with the gift of being able to see both sides of an issue.

the heart line

This line can help explain our attitudes toward romance and intimacy. It might even predict our future relationships!

• If the line is clear and deep, you're a loving, affectionate chica!
• If the line is weak or broken up, you may be in for a few future heartaches.
• If the heart line is stronger than the head line—you guessed it—your heart rules your head!

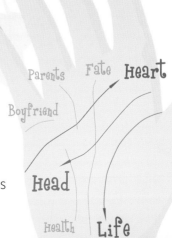

Sweet Fortunes

THIS GAME HAS ABSOLUTELY NO SCIENTIFIC BASIS, but your guests will find it fun to eat the evidence of their futures! Dump a bunch of colored candies, such as Skittles or Smarties, into a bowl. Have each girl grab a handful to examine. Each color carries its own prediction. The more of each color candy a girl has, the more likely her prediction will come true.

Color Guide:
- *Yellow*: Something good is coming your way. Your optimism and hard work is paying off!
- *Orange*: It's time for adventure. Get ready to do something you've never done before!
- *Red*: You're feeling mad or very passionate about something. Release some of your emotions, and feel better.
- *Purple*: You're going to be given an award or some sort of recognition in the near future.
- *Green*: For the next few weeks, you're going to be one cool cucumber, no matter what life throws at you!

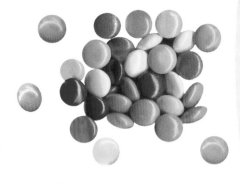

If everyone is too impatient to wait 10 years, you'll need an alternate plan. Make your predictions for the next year instead, and open up the time capsule in 12 months.

Making a Time Capsule

NOW COME PERHAPS the most accurate predictions of all: your own! Before the party starts, decorate a large coffee jar or any other sturdy container that comes with a lid. Label the capsule with your name and a warning: "Open in ten years!"

Once your guests arrive, ask each of them to write out a list of predictions for every girl in the room, including herself. Seal the lists in an envelope, and put it in the capsule. Throw in a few mementos of the year: the TV listings, a favorite magazine, and some school pictures. Seal your capsule, and store it in a safe place, such as a closet or attic. Now don't forget to invite your guests back in ten years. Together, you can see how accurate your predictions were!

SAYING Goodbye

SEND EACH GIRL HOME with a miniature Chinese take-out box (found at party supply stores). Fill it with fortune cookies as well as a small notebook in which they can write their dreams. Some say dreams can foretell the future. Why not add dream analysis to your next Fortune-Teller's Party!

Chapter 4

THE Hawaiian PARTY Luau

THE BACKYARD IS A PERFECT SETTING for this party, but you can transform your living or family room into a tropical paradise as well. Your guests will catch the island spirit as they learn the hula, do the limbo, and drink tropical "mocktails."

CHECKLIST TO SUCCESS

✓ **Three weeks before the party,** make your CDs of Hawaiian music, and hand out your invitations. (Page 26)

✓ **Five days before the party,** gather all the party decorations and supplies. (Page 26)

✓ **Three days before the party,** go on-line and find your guests' names in Hawaiian. (Page 28)

✓ **The day before the party,** shop for ingredients for your Fruit Kabobs and Coconut Pie. Don't forget to pick up some rice and sushi, as well as any other munchies on your menu. (Page 27)

✓ **The night before the party,** make the icy fruit lei for the Aloha Punch. Also whip up the Coconut Pie, and place it in the freezer.

✓ **The morning of the party,** decorate your house or yard. Make your Fruit Kabobs, and refrigerate.

✓ **Right before the guests arrive,** make the Aloha Punch—don't forget to slip in the fruit lei. Now you're ready to party, Hawaiian style!

WHAT'S *Your* ISLAND IQ?

Does "Maui" test your knowledge of Hawaii? Say "aloha" to this quick little quiz, and find out how much you really know about this beautiful state!

1 Hawaii is made up of how many islands?

a. 7
b. 8
c. 25

2 Hawaii is famous for producing...

a. tobacco and dates.
b. macadamia nuts and orchids.
c. lumber and lemons.

3 When did Hawaii become a state?

a. 1929
b. 1959
c. 1999

4 On which island would you find the city of Lahaina?

a. The Big Island
b. Maui
c. Kauai

5 What does the Hawaiian word "maholo" mean?

a. How are you?
b. Thank you.
c. Nice weather we're having.

6 Which Hawaiian island used to be a leper colony?

a. Lanai
b. Molokai
c. Maui

7 What is the name of the active volcano on Hawaii's Big Island?

a. Kakawawa
b. Kilauea
c. Killer Mountain

8 Hawaii was the ____ state admitted to the union.

a. 21st
b. 50th
c. 49th

Read on to pick up more than fun!

Answers:
The correct answer for each question is b.

25

Catch Island Fever and come to a

Hawaiian Luau

where paradise is a state of mind

When: March 2, 4 – 8 p.m.
Where: Elizabeth's private
beach getaway at 1234 Main St.

RSVP: 777-7777
or e-mail Elizabeth
at lizjones@home.com

Vacation wardrobe:
As much tropical flair
as you dare!

TiP from a HOSTESS with the MOSTESS

Have a few Hawaiian outfits on hand for guests who forget to dress the part so they don't feel left out.

LET'S GET IT Started!

The Invites

HERE'S A FUN AND USEFUL invitation idea: make CDs of Hawaiian music and design a simple invitation as the CD cover. Download or design a picture of a palm tree, hula dancer, or beach. Then, invite your guests to join you on your exclusive island getaway with all the party details. These creative invites will help get your guests into an island mood before they even step inside your party.

◀ Here's a sample invitation you can follow.

The Setting

BORROW FROM these fun decorating ideas: round up all of your houseplants and move them to the party area. Decorate the dining table by first laying down a plain blue tablecloth, and then laying fish netting on top. Place whole pineapples and coconuts on the table. (If you can't find coconuts in your local market, you can make your own by stuffing brown paper bags with newspaper.) Add some small shells as well as fish squirt bath toys. And attach plastic flowers to the sides of the tablecloth with tape.

Some other Hawaiian-themed finishing touches include: tiki torches in the backyard, blow-up palm trees, plastic flamingos, wooden parrots, masks, brightly colored Mylar balloons, and beach-themed piñatas.

The Edibles

BEFORE YOU EAT, line up your guests and have them conga over to the food table.

fabulous fruit kabobs

For the menu, really "stick it" to your guests with pineapple, kiwi, and other tropical delicacies on a skewer!

To make fruit kabobs, cut a variety of fruits into large chunks. Spritz a little lemon juice on the cut fruit to make sure it doesn't turn brown. Alternate different fruits on the skewers. Some fruits to try: pineapples, watermelon, honeydew melon, cantaloupe, apples, oranges, bananas, kiwis, strawberries, papayas, mangoes, and grapes.

Serve your kabobs with some rice and ready-made sushi from the market. Also, place Hawaiian chips and macadamia nuts on the table in straw beachcomber-style hats.

wiki wiki tiki drinks (*wiki* means "fast" in Hawaiian)

Set up a tiki bar, and serve up some Aloha Punch. Pour into tall glasses with umbrellas and straws in tropical colors.

Blend all the juices together, and chill in a punch bowl. Before serving, add the 7-Up and the sherbet.

For a festive touch, make an icy fruit lei to float in the punch bowl: fill one-third of a Bundt cake pan with crushed ice. Then, place a layer of sliced fruit on top of the ice. Add more crushed ice. Next, stand slices of lemon, lime, and orange, upright in the ice. Fill the pan with cold water and freeze. When you're ready to use, place the pan in hot water for a minute or two, and the lei should easily slide out.

You'll need:
- 16 oz can of frozen orange juice concentrate
- 16 oz can of frozen limeade concentrate
- 1 quart pineapple juice
- 1 quart pineapple sherbet
- 3/4 cup lemon juice
- 4 quarts 7-Up

The Playlist

ANYTHING HAWAIIAN, natch. Check out this compilation of ten island musicians that won the 2005 Grammy (the first ever in this category!) for Best Hawaiian Music: *Slack Key Guitar Vol.2*. Or put on some classic Don Ho hits, such as his medley of the island favorites "Tiny Bubbles" and "Pearly Shells."

island coconut pie

You'll need:
- 2 tbsp sugar
- 1/4 tsp almond extract
- 8 oz Cool Whip
- 3 oz softened cream cheese
- 1 cup shredded coconut
- 9" store-bought graham cracker crust
- 1/2 cup milk

Stay cool with this no-bake, island-style treat!

Using a mixer (ask your mom or dad if you need help with this appliance), beat sugar with cream cheese until smooth. Gradually beat in almond extract and milk. Fold in Cool Whip and shredded coconut. Spoon filling into graham cracker crust, and then cover and freeze the pie for at least four hours. Remove the pie from the freezer half an hour before serving.

GAMES & *Activities*

Aloha Welcome

FIND OUT WHAT your guests' names mean in Hawaiian by going to **www.e-hawaii.com/fun/hawaiianname**. Write down each guest's Hawaiian name on a name tag, and give it to her as she walks through the door. Also, adorn your guests with paper leis (available at party stores), or give them materials to make their own. All you need are some fake flowers (with stems) and some floral tape. Simply have the girls wind the flowers together by the stems and attach their leis with tape.

Instead of handing out leis, you can give each girl a plastic or real flower to put behind her ear. But remember: placement is everything. According to Hawaiian lore, if you place the flower behind your right ear, you're single. If you place the flower behind your left ear, you've got a special someone. The logic behind this? The left ear is closer to your heart.

Hand Over the Hula Hoop

ANYTHING WITH the word "hula" in it is a natural for this party. Break the girls into two teams, and have the girls of each team hold hands. Give each team a hula hoop, and hang the hoop on the arm of the first girl on each team. When you call out "Aloha," the girl with the hoop must step through it and pass it to the next person without letting go of her teammate's hand. The next player does the same thing. If a player does let go of her neighbor's hand, the team has to start all over again. The team that gets the hoop back to the starting player first is the winner.

Do the Limbo!

ALL YOU NEED FOR THIS game is a stick (a broom handle works well) or a rope under which guests can dance. Two people hold the stick, and, one by one, guests dance under without letting it touch any part of their bodies. Start the stick high—five feet or so, and lower it after everyone has had a turn. The guest who can limbo the lowest is the winner! Don't forget to blast a version of the "Limbo Rock" as you boogie down.

Tip from an Over-the-Top gal

Want to be authentic? Try providing flowers (real ones or fake) that actually grow in Hawaii, such as orchids, hibiscus, carnations, birds of paradise, and anthuriums.

Dance the Hula

PUT ON SOME HAWAIIAN MUSIC, and let your guests "try their hands" at the ancient art of Hawaiian dancing. But first, have each guest make herself a grass skirt. It's simple: tuck strips of green crepe paper into the waist of your shorts or jeans, and you've got yourself a swishy skirt!

The basic step is called the *kahola* or *vamp*. Simply step to the right, then follow with your left foot. Repeat. Now step to the left, and then follow with your right foot. Repeat. As you move your feet to the right, extend your right arm, palm down, to the right side of your body and bend your left arm, palm down, in front of your chest. Do the opposite when stepping to the left. Don't forget to bend your knees and sway those hips!

Now, add hand movements to tell a story. Here are some basic "words":

- **Swaying Tree:** With your left hand, hold the right arm at the elbow while the right arm and fingers make a swaying motion

- **Love:** Cross your hands over your shoulders.

- **Sun:** Hold your hands over your head as if shaping a sun.

- **Speak or Sing:** Bring hands to your mouth, then move them outward.

- **Grass Shack or House:** Form a rooftop with your hands.

- **Mountain:** Raise your arms sideways palms facing away from you, one hand higher than the other; one hand is the peak of the mountain, the other the slope.

- **Ocean:** Roll hands over each other.

TiP from an IMPROV QueeN

No time to research hula steps for your guests? If you have room in your party budget, hire a professional hula dancer to teach your guests or rent an instructional DVD.

SAYING Goodbye

SEND YOUR GUESTS home with an inexpensive sarong they can tie around their waist. And remind them to take home their leis to help complete the look.

Chapter 5

THE SPY THRILLER PARTY

ARE YOU A FAN OF JENNIFER GARNER? Do you feel it's a national tragedy if you miss the latest spy thriller? If so, then this party's right on target! Bring your guests into the conspiracy with this undercover party. Who knows? Together, you and your pals might save the world from some evildoers' diabolical plot!

CHECKLIST TO SUCCESS

✓ Three weeks before the party, send out the invitations. (Page 32)

✓ Two weeks before the party, plan out the route of your treasure hunt. Think up and write out appropriate clues. (Page 35)

✓ One week before the party, write out the Mission Accomplished character clues. (Page 34)

✓ Four days before the party, gather the props and prizes that you will need for the party games.

✓ Two days before the party, go grocery shopping for all the ingredients on your menu. (Page 33)

✓ The day before the party, make your mystery cake. Store it in an airtight container.

✓ The day of the party, whip up the guacamole in the morning. You'll make the quesadillas right before the meal. Set the scene of the crime. (Page 32)

✓ Right before the guests arrive, bring out the ink pad, and let the spy thriller begin!

WHAT'S *Your* SPY-Q?

Can you place these authentic and fictional spies? Take this quickie quiz to find out. Remember, you're under oath now.

1 Who played Dr. Evil in the **Austin Powers** movies?

a. Robert Wagner

b. Mike Myers

c. Dana Carvey

2 In the old TV spy show "Get Smart," agent Maxwell Smart was also known as...

a. Agent 77.

b. Agent 86.

c. Agent 99.

3 Which of the following actors has not portrayed James Bond?

a. Sean Connery

b. Tom Cruise

c. Timothy Dalton

4 "Alias" character Sydney Bristow has a master's degree in...

a. Politics.

b. English Literature.

c. Biochemistry.

5 What does the CIA stand for?

a. Central Interactive Agency

b. Central Intelligence Agency

c. Criminal Intelligence Agency

6 Nathan Hale was an American caught spying on the enemy during...

a. World War II.

b. The Revolutionary War.

c. The Vietnam War.

7 Who starred in **The Bourne Identity** spy thriller?

a. Will Smith

b. Matt Damon

c. Brad Pitt

8 On the TV show "24" starring Kiefer Sutherland, the number in the title stands for...

a. Kiefer's lucky number.

b. the hours in a day.

c. Kiefer's code name.

Read on to pick up more fun spy clues!

Answers:
The correct answer for each question is b.

TOP SECRET

To: ALL HIGH LEVEL AGENTS
From: Headquarters
Re: Your mission, should you choose to accept it

What: Come to a SPY PARTY where having fun and hanging out with friends is a matter of national security! Solve crimes against our country and, while you're at it, save the world from destruction!

Where: Elizabeth's house
When: 1800 h to 2200 h (6-10 p.m.) on March 2

RSVP: To Elizabeth. This is classified information. Do not be seen or overheard. 777-7777, Lizjones@home.com

LET'S GET IT *Started!*
The Invites

TYPE UP THE INVITATIONS as if writing a memo to a group of spies, informing them of their next mission. Then give all the party details. Put the invitations in manila envelopes, and label them "Top Secret." (Don't forget that manila envelopes will require extra postage; weigh them before you mail them at the post office.)

◀ Here's a sample invitation you can follow.

The Playlist

PLAY THE SOUNDTRACKS to some classic spy flicks, such as the two *Austin Powers* movies and *Mission: Impossible*, as well as the theme songs from "Alias" and "24." Throw in some James Bond theme songs as well; for example, play "Live and Let Die" by Paul McCartney & Wings, "Nobody Does It Better" by Carly Simon, and "A View to a Kill" by Duran Duran. In addition, any jazz recordings will nicely set the spy scene.

The Setting

ON THE SIDEWALK or front porch, draw chalk outlines of bodies to make your home look like a crime scene. Further the illusion by roping off areas of your house with caution tape (available at hardware stores). This is also a clever way to keep guests out of certain areas of your home.

When guests arrive, have a stamp pad on hand. Fingerprint them as they walk inside to make sure they have "security clearance" to your party. Label each guest's fingerprints. You can use the fingerprinted cards as place settings when it's time to eat!

The Edibles

YOU NEVER KNOW when your spies may be sent down south of the border on an undercover mission. Get your guests in the traveling state of mind with this Mexican-style menu filled with a few surprises of its own:

cheese quesadillas with a twist

What's the twist? Beans! To make one quesadilla, spread a layer of beans over a tortilla, sprinkle with a layer of cheese, and then drizzle on some taco sauce. Top with another tortilla. Cover with a paper towel, and microwave for 1–2 minutes. Cut the quesadilla into wedges, and serve with extra cheese, taco sauce, and sour cream.

You'll need:
- 1 pack flour tortillas
- 1 can refried beans
- 2 cups cheddar cheese, shredded
- taco sauce
- sour cream

super easy, super delicious mystery cake

This chocolaty concoction will delight and surprise all secret agents with an unexpected "mystery" ingredient.

Preheat oven to 350°F. Grease and flour a Bundt cake pan and set aside.

Mix the first six ingredients with a mixer (if you need help with the mixer, ask your mom or dad). When the batter is well blended, stir in the M&M's. Pour batter into a Bundt cake pan, and bake for 50–55 minutes (or until you can pierce the cake with a toothpick, and the toothpick comes out clean.) Let the cake cool for 15 minutes. Dust with powdered sugar.

You'll need:
- 1 package devil's food cake mix
- 3.9 oz package chocolate pudding mix
- 1 cup sour cream
- 1/2 cup vegetable oil
- 1/2 cup warm water
- 1/2 cup M&M's
- 4 eggs

gutsy guacamole

You'll need:
- 2 ripe avocados
- 2 tbsp fresh cilantro, chopped
- 1/4 cup onion, minced
- 2 tsp garlic, minced
- juice of 1 lime
- 1 tsp salt
- 1 tomato, diced

Now you simply have to serve up some "killer" guacamole!

Remove the skins and pits of the avocados, and mash the flesh with a fork. Leave whole bits of avocados in—the guacamole should be chunky. Add the next six ingredients, using as much of the lime juice as you need, and mix well. Top the guacamole with diced tomato. Serve up with tortilla chips.

Tip from an IMPROV Queen

If you don't have any M&M's on hand, you can use Reese's Pieces or any other small chocolate candies as a substitute mystery ingredient!

GAMES & *Activities*

Mission Accomplished

AS EACH GUEST walks in the door, hand her a Secret Agent Identity written on an index card. She should show no one her card. Each girl's mission: Complete the task on the card during the course of the party without arousing suspicion. If another guest guesses her task, she's out! (You can then share her identity and mission with everyone else.) Anyone who manages to complete her mission in secrecy wins a prize at the end of the party.

Here are a few Secret Agent profiles to get you going. Have fun coming up with your own. ▶

Watch Your Back!

As an alternative to Mission Accomplished, give each girl the alias of a celebrity, such as Jennifer Garner. Pin the name of the star on her back so she can't see who she is. Her mission is to discover her alias by asking "yes" or "no" questions to other guests.

sally sad sack

Poor little Sally! She comes from a long line of spies dating back to the Revolutionary War when her great-great-great-great-grandmother, Paulette Revere, served under George Washington. But to the dismay of her parents, Sally can't hack it in spy school. She needs to complete her final mission if she wants to take up the family business.
Her mission: Learn the middle names of all the party guests.

polly perfect

Polly is tops in her class at the Spy Academy. She speaks 16 languages, is adept at 12 types of martial arts, and has memorized the "Complete Guide to International Spies Turned Bad." Her biggest accomplishment is totally annoying her classmates with her know-it-all attitude. But now her classmates have their revenge: they're sending Polly on a mission no spy has ever before been able to complete.
Her mission: Uncover the secret crushes of three party guests.

chatty cathy

This agent just couldn't shut up. No one's secrets were safe with her. As a result, she was banned to solitary confinement where her only companion was a chatty cockroach. But now, Cathy's been given a way out of prison. Complete the following mission and she can join her fellow spies once again.
Her mission: Secretly confiscate one item each from four guests. (Don't take something that will cause panic when missed. And remember to give the items back!)

The Hunt is On

THE CENTERPIECE OF YOUR PARTY can be a treasure hunt. Here's a "briefing" on how to host one:

The government is missing a pile of valuable treasures. Your spies need to recover the goods. If you have a large group of guests, divide the girls into two teams. Before the party, write up ten or more clues that will lead your guests around the house, backyard, and/or neighborhood. The final clue will be the missing valuables, i.e. prizes for each girl on the winning team, such as cute picture frames, scarves, hats, lip glosses, etc.

Here are some ways to make the clues challenging:

- Write a clue out backwards on poster board. Then cut the clue up into puzzle pieces, and put the pieces into an envelope. To reveal the clue, the teams will have to put together the puzzle and find a mirror to decipher the writing.

- Write a clue on white paper with a white crayon. Provide a colored marker with the clue. Scribbling over the paper will reveal the message. (But they have to figure that out for themselves!)

- Come up with a rhyme or riddle for a clue. For example, "What's soft and comfy but messy all over?" (Answer: Your unmade bed!)

- Write a clue in numeric code. Assign each letter a number. At the end of the clue, provide a translation key.

- Make a connect-the-dots picture that will reveal the hiding place of the next clue.

- Create a letter-scrambled clue with a one-line description. For example, your clue could be EGARGA. The description would read "A place to store cars." (Answer: GARAGE)

- Do an Alpha Spell. Give the letters of a word in alphabetical order. For example, if you've hidden the next clue in a dictionary, you would spell the clue like this: ACDIINORTY. As with the letter-scrambled clues, provide a one line description to help the teams out.

SAYING Goodbye

AS THE PARTY winds down, give every girl a sack with some spy gear to take home: a fake nose and mustache for those times she has to disguise herself, a small notebook to take down clues, and a pack of gum (a play on the word "gumshoe" which is slang for "detective"). And as they leave your home, ask your guests to stay alert. You never know what trouble may crop up in the future!

Chapter 6

THE ULTIMATE COOK-OFF CHEF PARTY

WHAT'S COOKING? A lot when you host a pizza and cookie cook-off! Nothing's more fun than gathering your best buddies in the kitchen and sharing some laughs, good-natured gossip, and recipes. So don't be shy; *mangia, mangia!*

CHECKLIST TO SUCCESS

✓ **Three weeks before the party,** buy the pizza boxes, and send out the invitations. (Page 38)

✓ **One week before the party,** take inventory of all your cooking tools and appliances. If you need more than what you have for the party, ask friends and neighbors to lend you the needed equipment in a week. (Page 38)

✓ **Two days before the party,** hit the market and stock up on all the cooking ingredients. Also shop for prizes and decorations. (Pages 39–41)

✓ **The day before the party,** pick up extra cooking tools from your friends and neighbors. Make the pizza and cookie dough. Refrigerate.

✓ **The morning of the party,** decorate the eating area, and set out all the cooking tools so you won't have to hunt for them during the party. Slice up your pizza toppings, and refrigerate.

✓ **Right before the guests arrive,** turn on some Italian opera to give your friends a dramatic welcome. Let the cook-off begin!

WHAT'S *Your* COOKING IQ?

How comfy are you in the kitchen? Are you in touch with your inner chef? Take this quickie quiz to find out.

1 If a recipe calls for a cup of butter, this translates to...

a. one stick butter.

b. one and a half stick butter.

c. two sticks butter.

2 Which of the following should you not put in the microwave?

a. Plastic wrap

b. Tupperware

c. Foil

3 What's a colander?

a. An alternative spelling for "calendar."

b. A type of potato peeler.

c. A strainer that drains out liquid.

4 If a recipe asks you to mince an onion, you should...

a. peel it.

b. cut it into large chunks.

c. chop it into very small pieces.

5 Why is it recommended to rotate a cake during baking?

a. To get all the air bubbles out.

b. To distribute the sugar evenly.

c. To make sure the cake browns evenly.

6 What should you put on cut fruit to stop it from turning brown?

a. Sugar

b. Salt

c. Lemon juice

7 When making pasta, what does al dente mean?

a. Slippery

b. Wet

c. Firm

8 When greasing a cake pan, what else can you use to ensure the cake won't stick to the pan?

a. Baking soda

b. Corn meal

c. Flour

Keep reading for more cooking tips!

Answers:
The correct answer to each question is C.

37

Recipe for PARTY

INGREDIENTS: 6 friends
Good food
Creative cooking
ideas

TO MAKE: Take Elizabeth's house on March 2, 1 - 3 p.m. Mix friends well in the kitchen. Throw in one cup imagination and one cup culinary expertise. Add a dash of homemade pizza, freshly baked cookies, and party fever. Eat and enjoy!

RSVP: Call 777-7777 or e-mail Elizabeth at lizjones@home.com

essential cooking party tools

- 2–4 cookie sheets
- spatulas
- wire racks
- measuring cups and spoons
- mixing bowls of various sizes
- plastic wrap
- rolling pin
- cookie cutters in different shapes
- mixer
- wooden spoons
- cheese grater
- knives
- tons o'cookie decorations—nonpareils, sprinkles, candies

LET'S GET IT Started!

The Invites

SEND OUT INVITATIONS on recipe cards, available in stationery and bookstores. If you want to go the extra step, you can also buy some individual pizza boxes from your local pizza parlor and hand-deliver the invitations in the boxes.

◄ Here's a sample invitation to follow:

The Setting

DECORATE THE DINING room with checkered tablecloths and drippy candles to imitate an Italian bistro. Before the party, stock the kitchen with all the ingredients you'll need to make pizza and cookies. And while no girl would normally be caught dead wearing an apron at a party, have a few on hand for those guests who are worried about trashing their outfits.

◄ Ask your parents if you need help using any of the tools listed.

The Playlist

CELEBRATE ALL THINGS Italian while giving your guests a taste of culture by playing an Italian opera or two. A few to consider: *La Traviata* and *Rigoletto* by Verdi, *The Barber of Seville* by Rossini, or *Madame Butterfly* by Puccini. Your guests may be surprised at how much of this music they've already heard before. And you might even find yourselves singing along with an aria or two!

The Edibles

THE EDIBLES ARE the main attraction of this party, but you'll want to pre-make this pizza and cookie dough.

pizza dough recipe

Here's a foolproof recipe for thin-crusted pizza that can't be beat. This recipe makes 6–8 mini pizzas. Depending on the number of guests you're inviting, you might want to double the recipe. There needs to be enough dough so each guest can make her own mini pizza.

You'll need:

- 1 tsp active dry yeast
- 1 tsp sugar
- 1 1/3 cup lukewarm water
- 2 tbsp extra virgin olive oil
- 3 3/4 cup bread flour
- 1 tsp salt

Combine yeast, sugar, and water, and stir. Let rest until foamy (about 5 minutes). Stir in extra virgin olive oil and sea salt. Gradually add flour until dough forms a ball. You can do this by hand, with a wooden spoon, or in the bowl of a mixer with a dough hook attachment.

If making by hand, transfer dough to a work surface and knead for 4–5 minutes until soft and satiny but still firm (add extra flour as needed to prevent sticking).

Alternately, leave dough in a mixer with dough hook, and mix on low to medium for 4–5 minutes.

Transfer dough to a bowl, and cover tightly with plastic wrap. Refrigerate. Let dough rise in the refrigerator until doubled or tripled in size, 8–12 hours.

TiP from an IMPROV QueeN

If you don't have the time, forget making the pizza dough from scratch the day before; just buy some pre-made dough from the market.

perfect roll-out cookies

You'll need:

- 2 sticks softened butter
- 2/3 cup sugar
- 1 large egg
- 1/4 tsp baking powder
- 1/8 tsp salt
- 1 1/2 tsp vanilla
- 2 1/3 cup flour

THERE ARE DOZENS OF sugar cookie recipes out there, but these are by far the best! (Depending on how many guests you're having, you'll probably need to double or even triple the recipe).

With the mixer, cream the sugar and butter, and then add the egg, baking powder, salt, and vanilla. Beat until combined. Add flour, and mix well. Add more flour as needed to form workable dough. Roll dough into a ball, wrap in plastic wrap, and chill for at least one hour. (You can chill this overnight as well. When you remove the dough from the refrigerator, let it sit for a half hour at room temperature to soften.)

Activities

basic pizza sauce

Ready to start cooking? Together, whip up this simple yet delish pizza sauce (makes about a 2 1/3–3 cups. Double recipe as needed):

You'll need:

- 1 28-oz can Italian-style tomato puree or crushed tomatoes, drained
- 2 tbsp olive oil
- 1 clove garlic
- a touch of sugar (if needed)
- Salt and pepper

Heat olive oil over medium heat and add garlic. Sauté until fragrant. Add tomatoes and sugar (if tomatoes are too acidic), and simmer until thickened. Season sauce with salt and pepper to taste. Cool before spreading on pizza dough.

Alternately, you can make an uncooked sauce by simply combining tomatoes, olive oil, salt, pepper, and sugar (if needed) in a food processor and blending for one minute.

toppings

While some guests are helping make the sauce, others can grate the cheese. Have several different types of cheese on hand, from mozzarella to Monterey Jack. Pre-slice your other toppings, or let your guests help out with the slicing and dicing—if you trust them with a knife, that is!

Here are some toppings you can provide. But don't feel limited by this list, as most anything tastes great atop a pizza.

You'll need:

- pepperoni
- artichoke hearts
- bell peppers
- fresh tomatoes
- fresh rosemary, basil
- mushrooms
- pineapple
- olives
- asparagus
- cooked chicken
- red onion
- broccoli

Pizza Pizzazz —and Prizes!

ONCE THE CHEESE AND TOPPINGS are good to go, preheat the oven to 500°F. Remove the dough from the refrigerator, punch it down, and divide it into small balls. Ask each girl to flour her hands. Lightly flour a flat work surface, and have each girl shape her ball into a thin, round crust.

Transfer the crusts onto a greased cookie sheet with a spatula (two or three crusts should fit per cookie sheet). Once the crust is on the sheet, your guests can add sauce, their favorite toppings, and cheese.

Bake the pizzas until the edges are gold, around 8–12 minutes, depending on how many toppings the girls put on them. Let the pizzas cool a few minutes.

Before anyone takes the first bite of their mini-pizza, cut tiny slices off everyone's creation, and let the girls determine whose pizza is the best with a show of hands. The winning girl's prize? A pizza cookbook or a free pizza coupon to a local pizza parlor.

Once the contest is over, you can finally dig in and eat. Serve the pizza with some cut veggies and dip. Buon appetito!

Cookie Extravaganza

AFTER LUNCH, "ROLL OUT" THE COOKIE dough—literally—and get set to do some decorating.

Preheat the oven to 350°F. Meanwhile, flour the rolling pin and cookie cutters to ensure the dough won't stick to the tools. Roll out the dough to about 1/4" thickness on a flat surface that has also been lightly dusted with flour.

Let the guests choose which cookie cutter shapes they want to use. Once they have finished cutting out the cookies, transfer shapes to cookie sheets with a spatula, and bake cookies for 6–9 minutes.

While the cookies are baking, make frosting.

best butter frosting

You'll need:

- 2 sticks butter, softned
- 1/2 tsp vanilla
- 1 1/2 cup powdered sugar
- 1 tbsp milk (plus more as needed)

Beat two sticks butter with vanilla in a small bowl with an electric mixer until creamy. Gradually add powdered sugar and milk. Add more powdered sugar or milk as needed to get the desired thickness of frosting.

Once the cookies have cooled, let the girls go wild decorating them with different colored frosting (easily dyed with food colors), different candies, sprinkles, and decorations.

TiP from a HosTess with the MosTess

Need to find the counter space for all those frosted cookies to dry? Stack them! Frost the rim of a paper cup and stick it in the middle of a paper plate. Arrange as many cookies as will fit on the plate. Put frosting on the other side of the cup, and stick another plate onto it. Repeat until you have a stack of three plates.

SAYING Goodbye

Send guests home with a small cookie tin filled with their cookies. Also slip in the pizza and cookie recipes for future reference. Maybe you can book them for a sushi cook-off next year!

Chapter 7

THE Before & AFTER Makeover PARTY

ARE YOU AND YOUR FRIENDS READY for an extreme makeover? Of course you look great just the way you are. But you can still have a blast experimenting with different makeup, hairstyles, and fashions. So get set to indulge in a little makeover madness. Then step back and admire your total transformations!

CHECKLIST TO SUCCESS

✓ **Three weeks before the party, design and send out the invitations.** *(Page 44)*

✓ **Two weeks before the party, call around to different charities, and decide where to bring the Fashion Swap leftovers.** *(Page 47)*

✓ **Four days before the party, shop for all the beauty accessories you'll need for the party and the parting gifts for your guests. Decide what items to include in your "Makeover Roulette."** *(Page 46)*

✓ **Two days before the party, go grocery shopping for all the ingredients on your menu.** *(Page 45)*

✓ **The day before the party, create your "Makeover Roulette" awards. Also clean out your closet so you'll be prepared for the Fashion Swap & Show.**

✓ **The day of the party, whip up the pesto. Refrigerate. Create the different beauty stations in your home.** *(Page 44)*

✓ **Right before guests arrive, take a final tour of your "beauty school," and get ready for some fashion fun!**

WHAT'S *your* HAIR, MAKEUP, AND FASHION IQ?

Does your knowledge of these subjects need a makeover?
Take this quickie quiz to find out.

1. If your hair is wet, the best tool to detangle without damaging is...
   a. a comb.
   b. any brush.
   c. a round brush only!

2. To make your hair shiny after you wash it, give it a final rinse in...
   a. cold water.
   b. hot water.
   c. warm water.

3. To remove product buildup from your hair, use a...
   a. clarifying shampoo.
   b. volumizing shampoo.
   c. baby shampoo.

4. A maillot is...
   a. a swimsuit.
   b. a shoe.
   c. a duck.

5. The most flattering jacket style for most figures is...
   a. one that hits your waist or knees.
   b. one that hits your hips.
   c. one that hits your thighs.

6. If you buy a dress with an empire waist, this means...
   a. the waistline begins right below the bust.
   b. the dress has a low waistline.
   c. the dress has no waistline.

7. Makeup doesn't come with expiration dates, but in general, you shouldn't keep makeup longer than...
   a. a year.
   b. two years.
   c. five years.

8. If a lipstick is labeled "matte," the lipstick...
   a. has no shine.
   b. is super shiny.
   c. is a neutral color.

Read on for more makeover madness!

Answers:
The correct answer for each question is a.

43

Ready for a change?
Join Elizabeth at a

Makeover Party,

and have fun discovering
your inner swan!
Learn new makeup tricks
and hairstyles, and take
part in a fashion show.

where: Elizabeth's house
when: March 2, 4-8 p.m.

R.S.V.P. call 777-7777
or e-mail lizjoneeshome.com

Please bring along some clothes and
accessories that you'd like to give
away for a fashion swap!
All unclaimed items will be donated
to charity

LET'S GET IT *Started!*

The Invites

PLAY WITH A BEFORE AND AFTER theme for your invitations. Ask your mom or dad to take a Polaroid or digital picture of you looking like a total frump. Throw on a dirty, rumpled shirt and ugly sweats. Pull your hair down over your eyes. Slouch and frown. This is you "Before." For the "After" shot, change into a dressy outfit, style your hair, stand up straight, and show off those pearly whites.

Reproduce and cut out the photos, and then glue them onto a plain piece of stationery, labeling them "Before" and "After." List the rest of the party details. ◀ Here's a sample invitation you can follow.

The Setting

DIVIDE A LARGE ROOM of your house into different beauty stations. If the room doesn't have a mirror, provide hand mirrors so your guests can check themselves out. Lay out fashion magazines so girls can get some style tips and inspiration. And make sure you have enough chairs for each girl to sit comfortably.

You'll also need a changing room or two—perhaps you can reserve the bathroom or use your bedroom. And you'll want to have many different types of makeup on hand, as well as a wide variety of hair accessories and products, such as bobby pins, elastics, headbands, hair spray, and spiking paste, to complete your "beauty school." Don't forget cotton balls and makeup remover for any "do-overs."

Before

After

The Edibles

CHOOSE A SIMPLE MENU that you can "makeover" from so-so to sensational. Here are a few ideas to choose from. (Any recipe can be altered to fit the theme!)

spaghetti with red sauce

Make it over by serving spaghetti with green sauce, also known as pesto.

Throw the first three ingredients into a blender. (If you need help using this appliance, ask your mom or dad.) Blend. Slowly pour 1 cup or so of olive oil through the feeder hole of the blender lid until the ingredients have a smooth—but not watery—consistency. Add more olive oil as needed. Presto pesto! Spoon sauce over hot spaghetti noodles, and serve the dish with French bread (made over into garlic bread, of course!).

You'll need:
- 2 cups basil leaves
- 2–4 cloves garlic (to taste)
- 1 cup grated or shredded parmesan cheese (optional)
- 1 cup olive oil
- salt as needed

plain old vanilla ice cream

Make over vanilla ice cream by serving it with different toppings and letting your guests make their own sundaes.

You'll need:
- whipped cream
- chocolate syrup
- sprinkles
- cookies
- strawberries
- bananas
- cherries
- nuts

The Playlist

PLAY A COLLECTION of songs that newer artists have remade, of course! Some to choose from: "Big Yellow Taxi" by the Counting Crows and Vanessa Carlton, originally sung by Joni Mitchell; "American Pie" by Madonna, originally sung by Don McLean; "Feel Like Makin' Love" by Kid Rock, originally recorded by Bad Company; and "The First Cut is the Deepest" by Sheryl Crow, originally sung by Cat Stevens.

Before

After

GAMES & *Activities*

Makeover Roulette

HERE'S A FUN way to get those creative makeover juices flowing. Put out four bowls. Label them Eyes, Cheeks, Lips, and Hair. Cut up small slips of paper, and, depending on the variety of makeup you'll have on hand, write down different style ideas for each category, such as "Green Eye Shadow," "Bronzing Blush," "Sparkly Lip Gloss," and "French Braid." Place one makeover idea in each bowl per guest. (I.e. each girl gets to draw four times to create a complete "look.")

Once the girls are ready to play, take some "Before" shots, and let the roulette begin! Have the guests draw slips from each bowl one by one. They must use the makeup or hairstyle suggested on their slip of paper.

After all the girls have made themselves over, have an independent judge (your mom, perhaps) crown one guest the "Makeover Queen" based on how expertly (or creatively) the guest executed her makeover. Or hand out several awards, such as "Most Sophisticated," "Most Colorful," or "Wildest 'Do."

Spin the Bottle

NO MAKEOVER is complete without giving your fingers and toes a beauty boost! Have some fun by playing Spin the (nail polish) Bottle! Arrange different colors of polish on a table in a big circle. Place one bottle of polish in the center of the circle. One by one, have the girls spin the bottle. The girl who spins must paint one fingernail with the indicated color. Make sure you offer a lot of bold, bright, and downright funky colors. Asking guests to bring polishes from their own collections will add variety to the game.

Tip from an Over-the-Top gal

For maximum variety, ask each guest to bring one or two different kinds and colors of makeup so you'll have many options. But spare your guests any germs! When swapping makeup, you might also swap bacteria. Make sure you and your guests are using only brand new makeup, and provide lots of disposable applicators—such as sponges, cotton swabs, and cotton balls—so girls can make up safely.

Fashion Swap & Show

ON YOUR INVITATIONS or in person before the party, ask your guests to clean out their closets and gather any clothing that they've outgrown or never really liked. Hats, shoes, socks, purses, and jewelry are also welcome. Ask them to make sure the clothes are clean and in good condition—these items should be good enough to give to their best pals.

Ask each guest to bring her stash of unwanted duds to your party. (Remind your guests to first check with their mom or dad before purging their closets. Or else someone's mom might literally want the shirt off your back the next day!)

Together, sort through the clothes and make piles of shirts, pants, hats, skirts, etc. Let the guests dig through the piles and take what they want. By the end of the swap, most of the hand-me-downs will have found new homes. Have some extra bags on hand so guests can store their "scores." Anything that's left over will go to the Salvation Army or other charities.

After you've made your selections, dress up in your new outfits and stage a fashion show. Crank up some strong music with a loud beat, lay a rug or two down as a runway, and let your guests strut their stuff. Now's the time to take those "After" photos!

TiP from an IMPROV QueeN

What if two guests desperately desire the same shirt or pair of jeans? One idea: Before the swap gets started, give each girl 20 pennies to bargain with. They can "spend" their pennies in case they get in a bidding war. Giving away pennies is not allowed! At the end of the game, all the pennies go back to the hostess.

SAYING Goodbye

SEND YOUR GUESTS home with a makeup bag filled with inexpensive but fun makeup and hair accessories. Don't forget to slip in their "Before" and "After" photos if you don't need to have them developed first.

Chapter 8

THE *Life's* a *Beach* PARTY

SURE, YOU COULD throw a beach party in the middle of summer, but what fun would that be? Instead, plan yours in the dead of winter, and put a little needed sunshine into your friends' lives! Transform your home into one *Endless Summer,* and as quick as you can say "beach, baby, beach," your friends will forget all about the gloomy weather outside!

CHECKLIST TO SUCCESS

✓ **Three weeks before the party, create and deliver the invitations.** (Page 50)

✓ **Two weeks before the party, go online to buy an assortment of colored sunblocks.** (Page 52)

✓ **Three days before the party, gather, buy, or borrow any beach supplies you'll need for decoration.** (Page 50)

✓ **Two days before the party, pick up all the ingredients you'll need to serve lunch and play games.** (Page 51)

✓ **The day before the party, bake the cookies and make your Jell-O fishbowls.**

✓ **The morning of the party, make the sandwiches and decorate the room. Set up a craft station for decorating the visors.**

✓ **Right before your guests arrive, put on your sunglasses, turn up the surfing tunes, and get ready to party!**

WHAT'S *your* SUN-SENSE IQ?

You probably know it's smart to wear sunblock when heading out for a day of fun, but how much do you really know about safe sunning? Take this quickie quiz to find out!

1 What does SPF stand for?

a. Safe Protection Factor

b. Sun Protection Factor

c. Save Pale Faces
(from burning!)

2 It's best to apply sunscreen...

a. only when you're going to the beach or lake.

b. every day, even when it's cloudy.

c. never, if you have a dark complexion!

3 If a sunscreen has an SPF of 30 it means...

a. you can stay in the sun for 30 hours without getting burned.

b. you can stay in the sun 30 times longer than normal without getting burned.

c. the sunscreen has 30 ingredients.

4 There are two types of rays that sunscreen filters out. What are they?

a. UVC and UVD

b. UVA and UVB

c. UVme and UVthee

5 Should you ever use a tanning booth?

a. Sure, they're totally safe.

b. No. The rays can do long-term damage to the deep tissue of the skin.

c. Only if you don't have fair skin.

6 How many coats of sunscreen should you put on for the best coverage?

a. One's enough

b. Two

c. Five or six

7 During which hours should you be most careful about how much sun you get?

a. Early morning

b. From 10 a.m. until 2 p.m.

c. Late afternoon

8 How often should you reapply your sunscreen?

a. Every hour

b. Every two hours

c. Once a day

Turn the page to get your beach party started!

Answers:
The correct answer for each question is b.

49

SURF's UP!

Come to an **INDOOR BEACH PARTY** and have tons of fun in the sun

at Elizabeth Jones's home
1234 Main St.

12-4 p.m.
Saturday,
March 2

Dress appropriately and bring a swimsuit!

RSVP in the bottle or call 777-7777 or e-mail Lizjones@home.com

LET'S GET IT *Started!*

The Invites

HERE'S A FUN-IN-THE-SUN IDEA for your invites! Buy small glass bottles with corks at your local craft store. Write up the details of the party on small pieces of paper. Slip the invites inside the bottles and seal 'em up. You can also throw in some sand (available at craft stores). You'll have to hand deliver these invitations, but the effort will be well worth it; your friends will be so impressed with your creativity!

◀ Here's a sample invitation to follow.

The Setting

PUSH BACK THE FURNITURE in one or two rooms (with mom and dad's permission, of course), and set up a total beach scene. Cover the floor with beach towels. Raid the garage for any sun umbrellas, and spread them out near the towels. If you have, or can borrow, some beach balls, blow them up to throw around the room. Cut out and paint pictures of fish and mermaids to put on the walls. Strew some shells and beach toys around. And in the center of the room, place a blue towel or tarp. This is your "ocean!"

For some incredible edible decorations, buy some plastic fish bowls and make blue Jell-O in them. When the Jell-O is semi-set, pour in some gummy fish to create underwater worlds. Place the fish bowls around the room. Any guest with an appetite for fish can eat the Jell-O later!

TiP from a HOSTESS with the MOSTESS

Make sure your house is well-heated. After all, you asked the girls to dress appropriately, which means that most are going to show up in shorts and sleeveless tops!

The Edibles

BRING OUT THE PICNIC baskets, and lunch on your beach towels. Dish up this beach-y menu onto paper plates with small beach shovels.

everything-but-the-kitchen-sink submarine sandwiches

These sandwiches are great to serve because they're so easy to make—just pile slices of turkey, ham, and different cheeses on sandwich rolls, and you're good to go.

Serve with chips and watermelon slices, as well as these two favorites:

classic chocolate chip cookies

You'll need:
- 3/4 cup sugar
- 1/2 cup brown sugar
- 1 cup butter or margarine (two sticks)
- 1 package milk or semi-sweet chocolate chips
- 2 cups flour • 2 eggs
- 1 tsp vanilla
- 1 tsp baking soda
- 1 tsp salt

No beach picnic would be complete without some homemade cookies. Just don't drop them in the sand!
(Ask your mom or dad if you need help using the oven or the mixer.) Preheat the oven to 350°F. Cream together the sugars, butter, and vanilla. Then add eggs and beat well. Add the flour, baking soda, and salt, and blend well. Mix in the chocolate chips. Spoon small scoops onto ungreased cookie sheets, and cook approximately 12–15 minutes. Cool and store.

lemonade

You'll need:
- 6 cups lemonade (made from a frozen concentrate or powder)
- 1 1/2 cup sliced strawberries

No day at the beach is complete without a refreshingly cool drink of lemonade! Try this twist on pink lemonade—it's red! Using a blender, blend the lemonade and strawberries until smooth. Your delish lemonade is now ready to serve!

To round out this beach picnic, serve a tasty pasta salad and some deviled eggs!

The Playlist

TURN ON THE MOST classic beach band of all time: The Beach Boys. Some top hits to include: "Surfin' USA," "Surfer Girl," "Surfin' Safari," and "Good Vibrations." Two other 60s groups to program into your playlist: The Surfaris (their biggest hits were "Wipeout" and "Surfer Joe") and the clean-cut duo Jan and Dean of "Surf City" and "Ride the Wild Surf" fame. Also check out the surf rock group The Ventures. One album to try: *The Ventures Play the Greatest Surfin' Hits of All Time.*

Beat The Heat

WHEN THE SUN IS BROILING, a girl needs a little protection. Buy each guest a plastic visor to decorate (available at craft stores). Have on hand puffy paints in assorted colors, beach stickers, permanent magic markers, small shells, and craft or fabric glue. Your guests can wear the visors during the party and then save them for the summer.

Gone Fishing

DUMP A BOWLFUL OF GOLDFISH-SHAPED crackers onto your "ocean" and pass out a stick pretzel to each girl. They're going fishing! How do the girls reel in a fish? Pass around a bowl of peanut butter, and have girls scoop some on the ends of their fishing poles as "bait" to pick up fish.

To make the game move faster, set a timer and see, for example, how many fish each girl can pick up in thirty seconds. Play several times. The girl who catches the most fish in total wins a prize.

Winning girl's prize: A brand-new jar of peanut butter!

The Crab Walk

WHICH OF YOUR pals is truly the crabbiest? Find out by playing the crabwalk relay. To play:

- Mark a starting and ending line. Divide the party guests into two teams, forming two lines.
- Ask the first player on each team to get into the crab position—on their hands and feet, arching belly up. Next, gently balance a shoe on their stomach.
- On "go," each girl crab walks as quickly as possible from the starting line to the ending line and back. If her shoe falls off, she has to start over. Once she completes the track, the next person in line crab walks with the shoe.
- The first team to get all girls back over the starting line wins. Winning team's prize: A set of inexpensive seafood crackers!

Tip from an Over-the-Top gal

Think your friends could look a little more beach-bound? Nothing brightens a gal's complexion in the depth of winter like a tube of brightly colored sunblock. Pass some out to your guests, and let them make up each other's faces.

Colored sunblock might be hard to find during the winter, but companies such as Zinka, Inc. sell their products online throughout the year.

Swimsuit Competition

THERE SHE IS, MISS PALE AMERICA... No one expects you to have a tan in the middle of winter. But still, there's pale and then there is flat-out pasty! Invite your guests to participate in a tongue-in-cheek "I'm so Pale" competition.

First, give each girl a notebook and a pen or pencil for note taking. Next, create a fashion runway by laying down a long rug (or several beach towels) and lining it with your sand buckets, sand shovels, beach balls, etc.

Ask each girl to put on her swimsuit (or a pair of shorts for the modest) and take a stroll up and down the catwalk. As each girl models, everyone else rates her pale factor on a scale of 1–10 (ten being the most pale). Once all the girls have modeled, take a vote on who is the fairest of them all with a show of hands.

The winning girl's prize: A tube of sunless tanning lotion!

The Life Savers Drill

THE OCEAN may be too cold to swim in, but that doesn't mean you shouldn't be practicing your lifesaving skills for the summer. Here's a fun relay game you play with tooth-picks and packs of your favorite flavored Life Savers candies:

- Divide your guests into two groups, and form two lines.
- Give each player a toothpick and the first player in each line a Life Savers candy.
- On "go," each player, starting with the first in line, must transfer the candy behind her back from her toothpick to the toothpick of the girl behind her without touching the candy with her hands.
- If the candy falls to the ground, it goes back to the first girl in line.
- The first team to successfully carry their candy to the end of the line and back to the front again wins!

The winning team's prize: Packs of Life Savers, of course!

SAYING Goodbye

SEND YOUR GUESTS home with a beach bag stuffed with a few beach essentials, such as a beach ball, sun stick, and inexpensive flip-flops. They'll flip over their goodies. And the gifts will make stepping back into the cold a lot more palatable!

Chapter 9

THE Crafty Scrapbooker's PARTY

GET OUT YOUR SLEEPING BAGS—the gang's coming over for an all-nighter. While your guests may not get much shut-eye, they will come away with beautiful scrapbooks and plenty of fun memories to treasure.

CHECKLIST TO SUCCESS

✓ **Three weeks before the party, send out the invitations.** (Page 56)

✓ **A week before the party, shop for scrapbooking and other party supplies. Don't forget to pick up a scrapbooking album for yourself!** (Page 58 & 59)

✓ **Two days before the party, do all the food shopping for midnight snacks and other goodies.** (Page 57)

✓ **The day before the party, make a trip to your local video store, and rent the movies you're going to screen.** (Page 57)

✓ **The morning of the party, make the Chocolate Chip Banana Bread. You can also make the Chocolate Popcorn ahead of time and store it in plastic bags.**

✓ **The afternoon of the party, clear out a room for your friends to sleep in, set out the scrapbooking supplies, and you're all set for the party to start!**

WHAT'S *Your* SLEEP IQ?

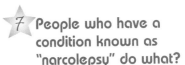

At some point during the night, most of your guests will eventually fall asleep—if only for a few hours! But how much do you know about the ABZzzs of sleep? Take this quickie quiz to find out.

1 How many hours of sleep do teens need every night?

a. 7

b. 10

c. 9

2 During which stage of sleep are you most likely to dream?

a. The non-REM stage.

b. The MEM stage.

c. The REM stage.

3 How often do you dream?

a. A few times a week.

b. Every other night.

c. Every night.

4 What does it mean if you have insomnia?

a. You sleepwalk.

b. You talk in your sleep.

c. You can't fall asleep.

5 If you're in bed and can't fall asleep, what's the thing to do?

a. Count sheep.

b. Turn on the TV.

c. Get out of bed for 15 minutes or so, do a quiet activity, and then try again.

6 Teenagers tend to...

a. stay up later and get up earlier.

b. tire easily

c. stay up later and sleep in later.

7 People who have a condition known as "narcolepsy" do what?

a. Have trouble falling asleep.

b. Don't need to sleep.

c. Fall asleep a lot.

8 If you dream your teeth fall out, experts say a common meaning may be that you're...

a. mad at someone.

b. feeling very sad.

c. embarrassed about something.

Read on for more sleepover fun!

Answers:
The correct answer for each question is C.

Catch up on your beauty sleep, because you are invited to a

Scrapbooking Sleepover Party

at Elizabeth's home
1234 Main St.

From 6 p.m.,
Sat., March 2
To 10 a.m.,
Sun., March 3

Pack your wackiest PJs and silliest slippers, a sleeping bag and a pillow. Please also bring 10 – 20 of your favorite photos to put in a scrapbook. All other scrapbooking materials will be provided.

or e-mail lizjones@home.com

RSVP to Elizabeth 777-7777

LET'S GET IT Started!

The Invites

TRY THIS IDEA: TAKE A PHOTO of yourself with some party props, such as a sleeping bag or popcorn, and arrange the photos on a piece of paper as if you were making a scrapbook page. Write down all the party info, then color photocopy your invitations, and mail them out.

◀ Here's a sample invitation you can follow.

★ It's a Party!

TiP from an IMPROV QUEEN

If you don't want to worry about having to serve dinner, start your party later in the evening. You can still serve fun snacks all night and breakfast in the morning, so it's not like your guests will be cheated of your fab cooking!

The Setting

RESERVE A PLACE FOR YOUR GUESTS to roll out their sleeping bags, such as the family room or living room. Make sure the room has a TV and a VCR or DVD player, because no sleepover is complete without screening a few flicks!

If you're throwing a summer bash, you can set up tents in the backyard and give guests their tent assignments as they walk through the door. You can even show movies outside with a portable DVD player or by setting up the TV/VCR on the back porch.

As well, you'll need one big table or a few smaller ones where girls can sit down to scrapbook. Have a few plastic storage bins on hand where you can stash all the supplies. This makes it easy for the girls to find everything they need.

The Edibles

SET UP A CONCESSION stand in the kitchen or outside where your guests can help themselves to snacks and drinks during the movie portion of the evening.

chocolate popcorn

For late-night noshing, perk up plain popcorn by catering to chocolate lovers with this fun and delicious recipe:

On the stove top, melt the butter, chocolate chips, and marshmallows in a saucepan. Add water, stirring constantly until smooth (ask your mom or dad if you need help with this). Mix popcorn and peanuts in a large bowl, and pour chocolate over the popcorn mixture. Let cool, and then dig in!

You'll need:

- 3 cups popped popcorn
- 1 cup milk chocolate chips
- 12 large marshmallows
- 1 cup salted peanuts
- 2 tbsp butter
- 1 tbsp water

chocolate chip banana bread

This is a morning recipe chocolate lovers will adore:

Preheat oven at 350°F. Grease a 9" x 5" loaf pan.

Using a mixer, beat butter and sugar until creamy. Beat in the eggs. Add flour, baking soda, and salt to the butter mixture, and mix well.

In a separate bowl, combine bananas, sour cream, and vanilla. Stir this into the batter. Fold in chocolate chips. Pour batter into loaf pan, and bake for 55–60 minutes. Banana bread is ready when a toothpick inserted in its center comes out dry.

You'll need:

- 1/2 cup butter
- 2 eggs
- 1 cup sugar
- 1 1/2 cup flour
- 1 1/4 cup mashed ripe bananas
- 1/2 cup sour cream
- 1 tsp vanilla extract
- 1/2 cup mini chocolate chips
- 1 tsp baking soda
- 1 tsp salt

The Playlist

GOOD FRIENDS and good times go hand in hand with scrapbooking. Create a playlist that accentuates this theme. A few songs to consider: "Time of Your Life" by Green Day; "We are Family" by Sister Sledge; "In My Life" by the Beatles; "Lean on Me" by Bill Withers; "You've Got a Friend in Me" from the movie *Toy Story*, and "Celebration" by Kool & the Gang.

And don't forget to pick a theme for the evening's movie screening. A few examples:

- **Lindsay Lohan Retrospective:** *Mean Girls, Freaky Friday, Confessions of a Teenage Drama Queen.*

- **Zany Cult Favorites:** *Napoleon Dynamite, Bill and Ted's Excellent Adventure, Wayne's World.*

- **Teen Classics:** *Breakfast Club, Clueless, 13 Going on 30.*

Activities

Making Memories

DURING THIS PART OF YOUR PARTY, each guest gets the chance to make a mini-scrapbook using pictures that she's brought with her. The girls can organize their scrapbook chronologically (for example, showing the beginning, middle, and end of a vacation) or by theme (having a page for friends, one for school, and one for pets), depending on their selection of photos.

Provide each guest with a small scrapbook (6" x 6", containing ten pages or fewer). Or, if you can't find small scrapbooks at your local craft store, your guests can make them as part of the project.

To create the scrapbook, use two pieces of acid-free 8 1/2" x 11" card stock as the front and back cover. Buy some acid-free paper and allot 5–10 pages per book. Punch three holes in the front and back covers, as well as the inside pages, and thread ribbon or yarn through the holes to bind each book.

scrapbooking tools

Here are some of the supplies you'll want to stock up on for your party:

the basics

- Small scrapbooks or enough acid-free paper to make into scrapbooks
- Adhesives (bottled glue, glue sticks, mounting tape or squares, picture holders, etc.)
- Different types of paper (colored, patterned, decorative, or metallic)
- Scissors: small paper cutters or shape cutters
- An assortment of decorative pens

the decorations

- Templates (stencil-like patterns made out of paper or cardboard)
- Yarn and ribbons
- Stickers
- Rubber Stamps
- Die Cuts (pre-cut paper shapes)

TiP from an OveR-the-Top gal

While your friends are working, take some Polaroid or digital shots of the party, and make a play-by-play scrapbook of the fun. This is a great way to immortalize the event— and create a scrapbook all your own!

some scrapbook pointers

- Stick 'em up. Want an easy yet attractive way to attach photos to a page? Use stickers to hold photos down at the corners. Other adhesives that work well when scrapbooking: glue sticks, liquid glue pens, photo tape, and mounting squares.

- Crop it. Instead of using entire photos, crop them to get rid of extraneous elements, such as your brother's arm or half of your mom's face.

- Be a cut-up. Make the photos even more interesting by using decorative scissors that make designs, such as scallops, as they cut.

- Pop out photos. Mat photos on the page to make pictures stand out. Simply cut out an enlarged outline of the photo so that approximately 1/4" of the paper extends beyond the picture's edges. Pick a color paper that accentuates or complements a color in the photo.

- Get balanced. Give each page a central focal point—one large picture or three smaller ones grouped together, for example. As you add elements to the page, make sure that the top half of the page has as many items as the bottom half so your page doesn't end up looking top or bottom heavy. Also check to see that the white space on a page is evenly distributed.

- Express yourself with colors. The colors you choose for each page help set the mood. Creating a scrapbook of your summer vacation? Use colors that sizzle, such as orange and red. If immortalizing a winter trip, cool blues and greens capture the feel of the season.

SAYING
Goodbye

MAKE SURE EACH GUEST takes home her scrapbook. And before the girls leave, ask them to sign the party scrapbook. You're left with a unique and memorable memento of your party that you will always treasure—and one that your friends can always flip through when they come over!

Chapter 10

Hostessing 101

Even the savviest gal on the planet can run into a few sticky situations that she's not sure how to handle. To make sure your party is a complete success, here are answers to some of your most frequently asked questions!

Q How far in advance should I send out the invitations? And should I have RSVPs on them? It seems like no one ever RSVPs anyway!

A Send your invitations out three weeks in advance. This gives your friends plenty of time to plan for the party, but not so much time that they disregard the seemingly distant date.

Do include an RSVP because you will need to know how many people are coming to your party to plan accordingly. If a guest doesn't RSVP (you're right; a lot of people don't take the time these days), it's perfectly okay for you to call or e-mail your pal and simply ask if she's coming or not. Sometimes this is the only way you'll ever get a response out of some people!

If you're super anxious about everyone being able to make it to your party, you can always informally e-mail or call your guests before sending out the invitations and ask them to save the date.

Catch Island Fever and come to

Hawaiian Luau

where paradise is a state of mind

When: March 2, 4 – 8 p.m.
Where: Elizabeth's beach getaway on Main St.

Q A girl I don't like that much invited me to her party, and I went. Does that mean I have to invite her to mine?

A Yes. By going to her party, you made a gesture of friendship. And now it's only right that you extend an invitation back to her and treat her as graciously as you would any other guest should she end up coming. In the future, it might be a good idea to decline the invitations to parties of girls you don't like. This way, you'll stay true to your feelings and never be put in this position again!

Q I've invited girls from a few different crowds to my party, but I'm afraid they won't mix. Any pointers?

A It's easier than you think: simply break them up during the planned activities. For example, when organizing a contest or game, make sure girls from each group are split up onto different teams. Working together on a common goal is a great way for your guests to get to know and like each other. Another winning strategy: make some cool place setting cards, and mix up your guests by giving everyone an assigned seat for lunch or dinner.

Q A friend of mine won't come to my party if this other girl is there. Should I dis-invite the other girl?

A Think about it. That would be really hurtful to the other girl. As a hostess, your job is to make all of your friends feel included. If someone chooses not to attend the party for a personal reason, that's her choice. Why not tell your friend, "I will miss you, and I hope you change your mind." This way she'll know that she is wanted, but it will also be clear that you aren't willing to compromise on the guest list. Hopefully she'll see how silly she's being and wind up coming and having a great time!

Q What if the girls don't like the food I'm serving? Should I have back ups?

A You only need one menu for your party. Trust me, everyone will find something to eat. Maybe one of your picky friends will even try something new and find out she likes it!

The only time you need to serve special food is if a guest has a food allergy or cannot eat a certain foods due to cultural or religious beliefs. For this reason, it's a good idea to find out beforehand and adapt your menu accordingly.

Q How do you decide if you should have boys at the party or not?

A That's something only you—and your parents!—can decide. If your parents are okay with it, and a lot of your friends are guys, go ahead and invite some. However, do keep in mind that having boys around changes the dynamics of a party; it might cause some of the girls to feel more self-conscious than they might be otherwise.

Q One of my friends is a total drama queen! How do I stop her from taking over the party?

A Keep her busy! For example, give her a task, such as organizing the meal or a contest. She'll feel needed and important. And the more she has to do, the less time and energy she has for creating one of her famous scenes!

61

Q What should I do if one of my friends brings drugs or alcohol to the party?

A. Avoid this scenario beforehand by making it clear that your party is a no-drug/no-alcohol event. If someone does sneak drugs or alcohol in, tell her to get rid of it. If your friend doesn't cooperate, you have no choice but to ask her to leave. Her behavior is not cool. And, because of your age, her actions could land your parents in jail.

Q What can I do to prevent my parents from not hovering over me and my friends during the entire party?

A Why not have a chat with your mom and dad to come up with some ground rules with which you can all live? As tactfully as possible, explain that you and your guests need some space, and then ask your parents for their help. Most parents want only to make everyone aware that there are grown-ups in the house for reasons of safety and security. They probably aren't interested in staying around for every activity! Maybe mom and dad can show up at the beginning and end of the party (and pop in for cake and candles). Be straightforward and open to compromise, and your parents will respect your need for privacy!

Q What should I do if people I didn't invite "crash" the party?

A It depends on the kind of party you're throwing; there's a big difference between an intimate sleepover and an end-of-year bash! The decision is really up to you and your parents. If you think the crashers would make good additions to the party—and your parents are okay with adding to the guest list—invite them in (first considering if you have enough food and supplies to cover everyone). But if you don't feel comfortable having the intruders at your party, you can politely but firmly ask them to leave. It's your party.

Q What should I do if two of the guests get mad at each other? It happened last year at my birthday party, and it wrecked the event for everyone!

A Hopefully this won't happen again. Your friends are now a year older and more mature! However, if it does happen, simply pull the girls aside and gently tell them you'd like them to make up—at least during the party—so that they, and everyone else, can have a good time. When confronted directly like this, the two will most likely do their best to stop the feuding.

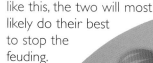

Q What should I do if a guest doesn't leave once the party is over?

A You can ask her, considerately, if she needs a ride home. If she says yes, you can then graciously offer your mom or dad to be her chauffeur!

If there is no clear reason why she isn't leaving, start cleaning up. This is an obvious signal that the party is over. And if the guest still doesn't get the hint, you can mention that you're pretty tired and want to get some rest.

Q What if a guest doesn't want to do any of the planned activities?

A Sometimes guests need just a little persuading to take part in the fun, especially if they're shy. Then once they do join in, they end up really enjoying themselves. So why not take the guest aside and ask her what her concerns are. Reassure her that you think she'll have a good time. If she still refuses however, don't force it. Make sure your friend is comfy where she is (get her something to drink, and offer her a cozy chair, for example), and let her participate from the sidelines. Also let her know that she can join in anytime should she change her mind.

Q What if friends volunteer to help me clean up after the party? Is it okay to make guests work?

A If your friends want to help, let them! Cleaning up after a party can be almost as much fun as the main event. It will give you and your pals time to talk about the party and re-live the highlights. And together you can get the house back in shape in half the time!

Thank you! for the cool candles!

Q Do I really have to write thank-you notes if I receive presents? It's such a drag!

A Thank-you notes may be going the way of the dinosaurs, but you can help revive good manners and bring them back into style! Keep the cards short and sweet, or make one computerized thank-you note that you can customize with a handwritten line or two. If you are really short on time, and your friends regularly check their e-mail, e-mailed thank-you notes will do the job nicely, too.

Conclusion

Hopefully, by now, your creative juices are flowing. You've got the basics of eight complete parties. Plus, you can mix and match ideas to come up with your own one-of-a-kind bash.

FOR EXAMPLE, why not borrow a few Hawaiian elements for your beach party? Or liven up your scrapbook party with some palm reading or a cookie-bake? Or steal some of the fun facials in the spa chapter for your makeover get-together? It's your party—go ahead and give it a personal touch!

And feel free to elaborate on any of the activities and games presented here. Use your wits to make them harder, simpler, wackier, or tackier—whatever suits you and your guests.

But most of all, don't stress. You've already got what it takes to throw a great bash: you! Just by reading this book, you've probably picked up dozens of hostess tips and tricks that will help put your guests at ease and make sure everyone has a blast. No matter what theme you choose, your party is bound to be a success!

So, are you ready to celebrate? Of course you are!

Then there's only one thing left to do... LET'S PARTY!